# Unofficial Tech Deck Skateboard Tricks:

*The Complete Handbook*

**Christopher C. Keller**

© 2018

# COPYRIGHT

**Unofficial Tech Deck Skateboard Tricks**

**By Christopher C. Keller**

**Copyright @201 By Christopher C. Keller**

**All Rights Reserved.**

The following eBook is reproduced below with the goal of providing information that is as accurate and as reliable as possible. Regardless, purchasing this eBook can be seen as consent to the fact that both the publisher and the author of this book are in no way experts on the topics discussed within, and that any recommendations or suggestions made herein are for entertainment purposes only. Professionals should be consulted as needed before undertaking any of the action endorsed herein.

This declaration is deemed fair and valid by both the American Bar Association and the Committee of Publishers Association and is legally binding throughout the United States.

Furthermore, the transmission, duplication or reproduction of any of the following work, including precise information, will be considered an illegal act, irrespective whether it is done electronically or in print. The legality extends to creating a secondary or tertiary copy of the work or a recorded copy and is only allowed with express written consent of the Publisher. All additional rights are reserved.

The information in the following pages is broadly considered to be a truthful and accurate account of facts, and as such any inattention, use or misuse of the information in question by the reader will render any resulting actions solely under their purview. There are no scenarios in which the publisher or the original author of this work can be in any fashion deemed liable for any hardship or damages that may befall them after undertaking information described herein.

Additionally, the information found on the following pages is intended for informational purposes only and should thus be considered, universal. As befitting its nature, the information presented is without assurance regarding its continued validity or interim quality. Trademarks that mentioned are done without written consent and can in no way be considered an endorsement from the trademark holder.

# Table of Contents

What Are Toy Tech Decks? ..................................8
Getting Started ...........................................10
   Build Your Own Finger Skate Park ..............11
Flat and Flip Tricks .....................................14
   360° Spin .............................................15
   Basic Kickflip ......................................16
   Nose Manual ........................................17
   Super Flip ...........................................17
   Fakie ..................................................18
   Front Uni-Wheeler ..............................19
   Rear Uni-Wheeler ...............................19
   Ollie ...................................................20
   Nollie ..................................................21
   Ollie North .........................................22
   Super Ollie .........................................23
   Shove It .............................................24
   360 Shove-It .......................................25
   Impossible .........................................26
   Your Mom ..........................................27
   Taco Flip ............................................28

- Air Walk ................................................. 29
- Board Twitch ........................................... 30
- Walk the Dog .......................................... 31
- Bandit Flip .............................................. 32
- Space Walk ............................................. 33
- Big Spin .................................................. 34
- Typhoon .................................................. 35
- Nose Grind .............................................. 36

Grind and Slide Tricks ....................................... 37
- 50-50 ....................................................... 38
- Board Slide ............................................. 39
- 5-0 (Tail Grind) ....................................... 40
- Nose Grind .............................................. 41
- Vietnam Air ............................................ 42
- Pinky Smith ............................................ 43
- Crooked Grind ........................................ 44
- Primo Grind ............................................ 45
- Nose Primo ............................................. 46
- Weak Grind ............................................. 47
- Hang Ten ................................................. 48
- Frontside Boneless ................................. 49

Grab Tricks ....................................................... 50

- Finger Stomp .......... 51
- Hand Plant .......... 52
- Christ Air .......... 53
- Sacktap .......... 54
- Madonna .......... 55
- Crossbone .......... 56

Verts and Ramp Tricks .......... 57
- Rail Walk .......... 58
- Gap Jump .......... 59
- Wall Ride .......... 60
- Superman .......... 61
- The Walk .......... 62
- Half Pipe Front Flip .......... 63
- Up the Hill .......... 64
- Helicopter .......... 65
- Pong to Pong Blunt .......... 66
- No Hands Vert .......... 67
- Plaster Flip .......... 68
- Back Stab .......... 69
- Nose Stall .......... 70

Conclusion .......... 71

# What Are Toy Tech Decks?

Let your fingers have all the fun with these mini skateboards designed for your fingers to ride. You can flip and do tricks, ranging from fairly basic ones to more complicated jumps and flips. This book will show you exactly what you can do and how to do it.

Fingerboards are built to around 1:8 scale and are designed to replicate real, full size skateboards. They were invented by Cameron Fox as a fun way to play and learn tricks without actually having to jump on a real skateboard. These little toys were actually a pretty big hit in the skateboarding industry, but later caught on with the general public.

Who doesn't love a fingerboard? Some of the original Tech Decks, with actual art from skateboard companies, are now collector's items. You can even find accessories for your Tech Deck, ready to decorate and add on to your fingerboards.

While there are some high end collectibles, most people just enjoy fingerboards for what they are, a great way to have fun. If you skateboard, you can use a fingerboard to work out tricks before you actually perform them with your feet, or you can just have a blast playing with the boards on their own.

In this book, you'll find all the tricks you can do with a Tech Deck. Some are simple enough to get right away. Others require quite a bit of practice. As you work through the tricks, you'll gradually gain confidence and ability and will be ready to tackle the tougher moves.

Good luck!

# Getting Started

Wondering how to start "riding" your finger skateboard? It's easier than you might think.

First, look at your pointer and middle finger as if they were legs. These are the two fingers you'll be using to skate with. The pointer finger will almost always be the forward finger, or the finger that is set at the front of the skateboard, while the middle finger will be the rear finger, or the one set at the back of the board.

Some people use a third finger, the ring finger. You can use this to make your tricks a little easier, but the

**Starter Position**

The basic start position is to place both fingers on the board, in the little divots right before the deck angles upward. On the official Tech Deck board, the front finger goes just behind the screws at the front of the board. The rear finger should be just behind the logo on the board. This is the position you will use in every trick, unless otherwise noted.

To move your board, you'll need to move your entire hand, of course. The tricks will be easier to do if you keep your non-skating fingers tucked back lightly.

You don't need to make them into a fist, but keep them out of the way.

If you want to start out with a fun mount, just set your skateboard on the table and put your fingers in the starting position on the table, as well. Then jump your fingers onto the board for a fancy mount.

## *Build Your Own Finger Skate Park*

If you want to go beyond the basic table moves, you're going to need some props. With full size skateboards, it's normal to head to the skate park, but if you're working with fingerboards, you can make your own.

### Rails

For actual rails, hit the hardware store and pick up some cupboard door handles. The long bar ones work perfectly when mounted on a flat surface, and will serve as a proper rail.

You can also build a low box out of plywood to make a sidewalk "rail" and even vary the heights. Paint it up with some graffiti for a cooler look. Dollhouse benches make an excellent park bench rail, too. Just make sure you mount them to a surface so they won't fall over.

## Stairs

If you need some steps, you can either buy dollhouse steps or make your own by cutting 1x1 pieces of board in half diagonally and mounting on a ramp. Alternatively, fold stiff cardboard and mount on a piece of wood.

Another option, if you want something that will last a long time, is to create a mold with cardboard and then fill it with concrete. You'll end up with some very solid stairs. It's a good idea to round any edges with a little sandpaper before you use them.

## Ramps

Create your own ramps with a piece of plywood that you attach to a block of wood. If you want something a bit more creative, you can create ramps that have varying heights.

Old sinks work well as pool ramps and can be set into a table where you set up your fingerboard skate park. Another option is to make your own "pool" by creating a mold in sand or plaster and pouring concrete to get the longer lasting design.

**Pipes**

The simplest way to make a pipe or half or quarter pipe is to get an actual PVC pipe and cut it to the size you need, then mount it against a wooden form to balance it. However, you can make a wooden one with some patience.

For a wooden quarter pipe or half pipe, you can either cut a solid block of wood to the right curves, or you can heat and bend a thin piece of plywood and set it into a curve with the box under it, cut to fit.

Don't forget to decorate your skate park, using paint, markers, and spray paint. Get creative and make it fun!

Now that you know the basics, you're ready to get started with some tricks!

# Flat and Flip Tricks

The tricks in this section are meant to be done on a flat surface, so you need absolutely no other equipment apart from your fingerboard and your fingers. These are the tricks you should start out with, since the basics will be what you use when you start to grind and use ramps.

Your surface should be flat and smooth enough to roll on easily. You want to avoid shiny or slippery tables, though, because they can cause the board to slip and slide when you're trying to do your tricks.

While a table works best for this type of trick, since you can sit at exactly the right height to manage everything, you can also do tricks on the floor, a counter, or just about any other surface that provides a flat option for rolling. We'll refer to this as the rolling surface throughout this book.

## *360° Spin*

This trick lets you spin your board in a 360° turn, with only one finger. It's fun and it looks pretty cool . . . plus it's easy to master quickly, which is why it's the first trick in the book.

**Step 1:** Plant both fingers in standard stance on your board.

**Step 2:** Tip the board back slightly, so the weight is on your rear finger.

**Step 3:** Use the front finger to push the front of the board hard to the left. Keep the rear of the board in place with the rear finger.

**Step 4:** Spin the board completely around and land your front finger on it again.

You just did your first trick! You might need a bit of practice to get the board to spin completely, but be patient and it will happen.

## *Basic Kickflip*

This trick has more steps, but it looks that much more impressive when you perform it! Basically, with this trick, you're kicking the board so that it flips completely around horizontally, landing just in time for your fingers to hit the deck. Ready to learn how to make it happen?

**Step 1:** Put your fingers on the board in the start position.

**Step 2:** Roll rapidly to the left. You need some speed for this trick, so get those wheels moving.

**Step 3:** Use your rear finger to hit the tail down against the rolling surface. The entire board should pop off the surface and fly into the air.

**Step 4:** Press on the board, moving your front finger toward the nose of the board and making it flip around. This step takes a lot of practice to get the pressure right. You need to apply it right on the edge of the board closest to you in order to get it to flip.

**Step 5:** Once the board has rotated completely, land your fingers on the deck.

**Step 6:** Use your fingers to move the board back to the rolling surface and brake the move.

## *Nose Manual*

You'll use this move in some landings. It's pretty simple looking, but it can be tricky if you're trying to land in this position. You'll need to learn to land without hitting the back wheels.

**Step 1:** Use any position you like.

**Step 2:** Press on the nose of the board with your front finger, just enough to lift the tail and have the board on the front two wheels only.

**Step 3:** Ease the pressure so the back wheels touch the rolling surface, too.

## *Super Flip*

Even if you don't have a full size skateboard yourself, you're bound to have watched this move. Now it's time to replicate the flip and grab in miniature with your Tech Deck.

**Step 1:** Put your fingers on the table or rolling surface, without touching the board. Ideally, your thumb will be behind your middle finger to give it extra support.

**Step 2:** Hit the tail of the board as hard as possible with your middle finger. The board should pop into the air and flip.

**Step 3:** Grab the board in the air with your usual fingers.

**Step 4:** Gently land the board with your fingers in position.

## *Fakie*

The word fakie just means backwards in skater speak. So, any fakie tricks will simply be reverse tricks of the original. This move, however, is fairly basic and you can master it in moments.

**Step 1:** Put your fingers in the starter position on the board.

**Step 2:** Roll the board backwards so that your rear finger acts as the front finger.

*Note: This is the beginning move for many fakie tricks, so master it until it feels perfectly comfortable.*

## *Front Uni-Wheeler*

A variation of the Nose Manual, this trick takes things a step further, so you're only balanced on one wheel. This is not a trick to hold for long, but it can be a fun way to add some interest to a regular move.

**Step 1:** Put your fingers on the board in any position you choose.

**Step 2:** Carefully move your front finger to the front and side, pressing to lift the board so it only balances on one front wheel.

**Step 3:** Gently slide the front finger back to ease the board to the rolling surface.

## *Rear Uni-Wheeler*

Just like it sounds, this is the opposite of the Front Uni-Wheeler. Again, it's something simple to master, but when you're in the middle of a bigger trick, it can be tricky.

**Step 1:** Start with any position you choose.

**Step 2:** Slide your rear finger back and to the side until the board is balanced on one rear wheel.

**Step 3:** Gently ease the board back to level by sliding your rear finger back into position.

## *Ollie*

This is one of the most basic tricks you can do on a skateboard, mini or not. It will be one of the earliest moves you learn on your fingerboard and is often the base of other tricks. You'll be using this for jumping over items and also for doing grinds, which we cover later in this book.

**Step 1:** Put your fingers on the board in the starter position.

**Step 2:** Without rolling, hit the tail of the board with your rear finger and it should pop up into the air. The whole board will go up.

**Step 3:** Slide your front finger forward on the board to level the board out.

**Step 4:** Bring the board back to the rolling surface or table and stop.

*Note: If your board isn't getting off the ground, you aren't popping the tail hard enough. Try to do everything in one smooth, flowing motion to get it up off the ground.*

## *Nollie*

Once you've mastered the Ollie, it's time to learn the Nollie, which is basically just the Ollie in reverse. Instead of popping the tail, you'll be popping the front of the board, which means you'll be reversing most of the steps in the above tutorial.

**Step 1:** Put your fingers in the starter position, but on the opposite side of the board.

**Step 2:** Use your front finger to pop the board up, by hitting the front down to make the back pop up.

**Step 3:** Slide the rear finger toward the back of the board to level it all out. At this point, the board will be in the air.

**Step 4:** Gently guide the board back to the rolling surface.

## *Ollie North*

Looking for a more impressive trick with the basic Ollie move? This is it! With this trick, you actually get the board into a vertical position for a split second. It can be tough to land, so you'll need a lot of practice.

**Step 1:** Put your fingers in the starter position.

**Step 2:** Hit the tail with your rear finger to pop the board into the air.

**Step 3:** Twist your hand toward your left, forcing the board to point straight up in the air.

**Step 4:** Twist back and bring the board back to the rolling surface.

## *Super Ollie*

You can really impress friends and family with this one, since it actually combines two tricks, the Ollie and the Kickflip. It requires plenty of practice, but it's well worth the effort once you manage to nail it.

**Step 1:** Put your fingers on the board in the start position.

**Step 2:** Roll rapidly to the left. You need some speed for this trick, so get those wheels moving.

**Step 3:** Use your rear finger to hit the tail down against the rolling surface. The entire board should pop off the surface and fly into the air.

**Step 4:** Slide your front finger forward to level out.

**Step 5:** Press on the board, moving your front finger toward the nose of the board and making it flip around. This step takes a lot of practice to get the pressure right. You need to apply it right on the edge of the board closest to you in order to get it to flip.

**Step 6:** Once the board has rotated completely, land your fingers on the deck.

**Step 7:** Slide your front finger forward and bring the board to the rolling surface, touching the front wheels only.

**Step 8:** Gently bring the board down to level and roll to a stop.

## *Shove It*

Spin your board after an Ollie to really make it look cool. This is a fun little trick that is actually fairly simple to do once you've mastered the Ollie. You should be able to learn it fairly quickly.

**Step 1:** Put your fingers in the starter position on the board.

**Step 2:** Pop the board in the air by hitting the tail with the rear finger.

**Step 3:** Slide your front finger forward to level out the board and pull your rear finger toward yourself sharply while in the air. The board should spin horizontally 180°.

**Step 4:** Land the board gently by guiding it to the rolling surface.

## *360 Shove-It*

Take the previous trick a step further by getting the board to spin in a complete 360°, rather than just 180°. There are actually further variations where you go for 540° or even 720°, but you need to really pop the board high in order to get those numbers.

**Step 1:** Put your fingers in the starting position on the board.

**Step 2:** Pop the board in the air by hitting the tail with the rear finger. You'll need to do this hard in order to get it high enough to spin completely around before landing.

**Step 3:** Slide your front finger forward to level out the board and pull your rear finger toward yourself sharply while in the air to spin the board a full 360° before you land.

**Step 4:** Guide the board back to the rolling surface to land. Your fingers should be in the same position as they were at the beginning of the trick.

## *Impossible*

There's a good reason this trick is called Impossible. It can be done with a lot of patience and hard work, though. Once you've managed to do this trick, you'll be set to put on a show!

**Step 1:** Put your fingers on the board in the starting position.

**Step 2:** Pop the board into the air by striking the tail with your rear finger, hard.

**Step 3:** Lift your front finger to let the board flip completely around the rear finger, nose over tail, with the finger in the middle of the flip.

**Step 4:** Get your fingers back on the board and land it.

## *Your Mom*

This trick requires using your entire hand and is one of the few tricks that has virtually nothing to do with actual skateboarding. However, it's a fun way to show off your skills and to put your whole hand to use.

**Step 1:** Put your fingers in the starting position on the board.

**Step 2:** Hit the tail of the board hard with your rear finger, popping it up into the air.

**Step 3:** Let the board do a half flip and then use the back of your hand to catch the board.

**Step 4:** Hold the board on your hand for a second, then flip your front finger up to swing the board back around. It should flip again.

**Step 5:** Put your fingers back on the board in mid-air.

**Step 6:** Land the board on the rolling surface and stop.

## *Taco Flip*

This trick requires a little prep and is a fun way to start off a round of tricks. It's pretty basic, but adds a lot of flair to your moves.

**Step 1:** Set the board on its side. The trucks should be facing you.

**Step 2:** Place your fingers on the side closest to you, on the rolling surface.

**Step 3:** Use your front or index finger to hit the board and slide toward you, flipping the board in the air.

**Step 4:** Jump your fingers onto the board and bring it back to the rolling surface to land.

**Step 5:** Roll the board into the next trick.

## *Air Walk*

Here's a neat way to do a basic jump and make it look different. This trick works on a flat surface, but you can also use it when jumping a gap or any other time you have the fingerboard in the air.

**Step 1:** Place your fingers in the starter position on the board.

**Step 2:** Pop the board in the air by hitting the tail with your rear finger.

**Step 3:** Use your index finger to level the board out in the air.

**Step 4:** Move your fingers in a walking movement on the board in mid-air.

**Step 5:** Place your fingers in the starter position again and land the board on the rolling surface.

## *Board Twitch*

While this is under the flat surface tricks section, you can also do it on a ramp, as you come off the ramp. It may be a good idea to perfect the whole thing on the ground before you start doing it with ramps, though.

**Step 1:** Put your fingers on the board in the starting position.

**Step 2:** Pop the board into the air by hitting the tail with your rear finger. Aim for a pretty high Ollie.

**Step 3:** Use your fingers to twitch the board to one side and back to normal.

**Step 4:** Land the board on the rolling surface again and roll into the next trick.

## *Walk the Dog*

Ready to take your dog for a walk? Nevermind, this is just a board trick that mimics walking your dog and then flipping around to go the other way.

**Step 1:** Set your fingers in the start position on your board.

**Step 2:** Roll the board slowly forward.

**Step 3:** Use your tail finger and press down, spinning the board 180°.

**Step 4:** Switch your finger placement and continue rolling.

## *Bandit Flip*

Having fun with your fingerboard is all part of the game and this particular trick is extra amusing. It uses moves you could never do with a full size board.

**Step 1:** Put your front finger under the board, immediately behind the front trucks.

**Step 2:** Make the shape of a gun with your hand and shoot your target. The board will hang from your finger.

**Step 3:** Move your front finger up quickly and flip the board.

**Step 4:** Land the board with both fingers on the deck.

## *Space Walk*

If you're looking for a quick trick to pick up, this is the perfect one to choose. It's relatively easy to master and can be pretty impressive when done smoothly.

**Step 1:** Put your fingers in the start position on the board.

**Step 2:** Start to roll along a flat surface at medium speed.

**Step 3:** Use your rear finger to push the tail down slightly, but not enough to hit the ground. The nose should be in the air.

**Step 4:** Use your fingers to swing the nose to one side and then the other as you roll along.

**Step 5:** Repeat the above motion as long as you are rolling.

**Step 6:** To land, simply level the board out by pushing the nose down again.

## *Big Spin*

Here's another fast trick to learn. It requires some dexterity, but you can easily pick it up in a few minutes.

**Step 1:** Put your fingers in the usual position on the board.

**Step 2:** Roll the board backwards at medium speed.

**Step 3:** Jump your fingers in the air, hitting the side of the board with your front finger to spin it 360°.

**Step 4:** Twist your hand 180° in the same direction as the board spins.

**Step 5:** Land your fingers on the board. It should now be going backwards, with your fingers facing forward.

## *Typhoon*

This trick is really similar to the Ollie, but a little different in that it is less predictable. You can't really control this trick, so it's a surprise every time.

**Step 1:** Put your fingers on the deck in the starting position.

**Step 2:** Hit the rear corner of the board to send the board flipping into the air. It won't move in a predictable manner, so it can be difficult to figure out where it will land.

**Step 3:** Once you know which way the board is going, jump your fingers and land in the start position on the board, bringing it to the rolling surface again.

## *Nose Grind*

This

**Step 1:** Put

**Step 2:** Roll

**Step 3:** Hit

**Step 4:** Use

**Step 5:** Grind

**Step 6:** To

**Step 7:** Land

# Grind and Slide Tricks

Grinding is when you slide your board along a surface using the trucks of the skateboard. It's called grinding because you are literally grinding parts of the board against a hard surface. You will usually do this against a rail, which may be an actual rail or it could be something less obvious, like a curb.

Since you are going to be hard pressed to find a tiny staircase, curb, or sidewalk to grind, you'll either need to invest in specialty equipment or come up with your own variations.

You can create your own rails by using things like solid boxes, books, or even the corner of a table. These are great makeshift options until you have your own skate park built for your fingerboards. Alternatively, you can buy your own miniature skate park accessories, as there are companies that sell them.

## *50-50*

When you're starting out with grinding, you'll want to begin with this trick. It lets you get used to the feel of the game and eventually, you can build up to the more complicated tricks. The upside of these moves is that you don't have to worry about breaking a leg.

**Step 1:** Put your fingers on the board in the starter position.

**Step 2:** Roll toward your rail at moderate speed.

**Step 3:** Hit the tail lightly with your rear finger to pop the board up in the air, just high enough to land on the rail.

**Step 4:** Use your front finger to level the board so that both trucks land on the rail.

**Step 5:** Use your momentum to slide down the rail.

**Step 6:** Pop the board in the air again by hitting the tail with the rear finger and land it on the flat rolling surface.

## *Board Slide*

While grinding almost always involves using the trucks to slide, this particular trick uses the actual board. Be careful not to land too hard, since it could break your board, depending on how much pressure you put on the board as you do the trick.

**Step 1:** Put your fingers on the board in the starting position.

**Step 2:** Roll rapidly toward your rail.

**Step 3:** Use your rear finger to hit the tail and pop the board into the air.

**Step 4:** Use your front finger to slide forward and level the board out, while twisting slightly so that the actual board comes into contact with the rail. The trucks should be on either side of the rail.

**Step 5:** Slide along the rail as far as you like before popping the board into the air again.

**Step 6:** Land safely on the rolling surface.

## *5-0 (Tail Grind)*

There are endless variations to grinding, but this one is a pretty basic one. Here, you'll grind with only the back truck of the fingerboard. This is slightly more complicated than the 50-50, but not much more.

**Step 1:** Put your fingers on the board in the starter position.

**Step 2:** Roll toward the rail at moderate speed.

**Step 3:** Use your rear finger to hit the tail and pop the board into the air.

**Step 4:** Don't use your front finger to level the board, instead, let the back truck hit the rail.

**Step 5:** Grind along with the nose of the board in the air, using only the rear truck.

**Step 6:** Twist the board and press the nose down to lift the tail off the rail.

**Step 7:** Use both fingers to land the board carefully on the rolling surface.

## *Nose Grind*

This trick is the opposite of the 5-0. It requires using the front truck to grind, rather than the rear, which can be a little more difficult to achieve.

**Step 1:** Put your fingers on the board in the starter position.

**Step 2:** Roll toward the rail at moderate speed.

**Step 3:** Hit the tail of the board with your rear finger to pop the board into the air, moderately high.

**Step 4:** Use your front finger to press the nose of the board down and to land on the rail, on the front truck only. Keep the tail in the air.

**Step 5:** Grind along the rail for as far as you want.

**Step 6:** To dismount, use your rear finger to twist the tail over and hit it to pop the nose into the air.

**Step 7:** Land the board on the rolling surface.

## *Vietnam Air*

This trick combines spinning and jumping with grinding for a truly impressive trick that you'll need to practice quite a bit to make sure it actually works. It's a tougher one, but well worth learning.

**Step 1:** Put your fingers on the board in the starter position.

**Step 2:** Roll toward your vert at a regular speed.

**Step 3:** When you hit the edge of the vert, hit the tail of the board with your rear finger to flip it up onto your middle fingers.

**Step 4:** Spin the board around your middle finger as many times as you like (3 times is the norm).

**Step 5:** Flip your fingers back on top of the board and land it on the grinding mechanism with the tape side down.

**Step 6:** Use your two riding fingers to flip the board by lifting the board by the trucks and flicking it.

**Step 7:** Land your fingers on the deck and roll away.

## *Pinky Smith*

Here's a good, easy trick that just varies from previous ones and gives it a little twist and flare by getting your pinky finger involved.

**Step 1:** Place your fingers in the normal start position on the board.

**Step 2:** Roll forward toward the rail at medium speed.

**Step 3:** Hit the tail with your rear finger to pop it in the air.

**Step 4:** Land on the rail with only your pinky finger on the back screws. The front of the board should hang off the side.

**Step 5:** Grind along smoothly.

**Step 6:** To dismount, lift your pinky and hit the tail with your rear finger.

**Step 7:** Land with your usual fingers in place.

## *Crooked Grind*

Get creative with a little movement as you go on this grind. You can use any regular rail for it, low or high, and make it wobbly.

**Step 1:** Put your fingers on the board in the starter position.

**Step 2:** Roll quickly toward your rail.

**Step 3:** Pop the board into the air by hitting the tail with your rear finger.

**Step 4:** Slide your front finger forward until the board is tilted somewhat downward and land on the rail with the front truck.

**Step 5:** Grind and wiggle your hand so that the board does a crooked grind.

**Step 6:** Use your rear finger to swing the tail of the board off the rail and pop the front into the air with your front finger hitting the nose.

**Step 7:** Land with both fingers on the board.

## *Primo Grind*

You can have a lot of fun with this particular trick, but it works best on higher rails, like those for stairs, fences, etc. It does NOT do well on a low curb or similar, since you need room for the edge of the board.

**Step 1:** Put your fingers on the board in the usual start position.

**Step 2:** Roll quickly toward the rail. You'll need some speed for this one.

**Step 3:** Pop the tail with your rear finger to lift the board.

**Step 4:** Twist the board slightly in midair so that it hits the rail perpendicular to the ground. The side of front and rear wheels should be on the rail.

**Step 5:** Grind along the rail, with the front and rear wheel being the grinding surface.

**Step 6:** Tip off the rail by tilting your fingers.

**Step 7:** Land flat with both fingers in the usual position.

## *Nose Primo*

A cool variation of the original primo grind, this one uses only the front wheels to keep you going.

**Step 1:** Put your fingers on the board in the start position.

**Step 2:** Head toward the rail with quite a bit of speed.

**Step 3:** Hit the tail with your rear finger to pop into the air.

**Step 4:** Twist your fingers and use the front to push the nose of the board down a little. The board should land on the front wheel only.

**Step 5:** Grind along with the front wheel only.

**Step 6:** Dismount by tipping the board over with your fingers and leveling it out as you drop.

**Step 7:** Land with both fingers in the usual position.

## *Weak Grind*

While it might sound, well, weak, this trick actually requires more finesse than your average grind. You'll need to get the angles just right to make it work.

**Step 1:** Place your first two fingers in the usual starting position on your board.

**Step 2:** Roll toward your rail quickly.

**Step 3:** Use your rear finger to hit the tail of the board and pop it up in the air.

**Step 4:** Level out the board with your front finger.

**Step 5:** Land on the rail with the rear truck and keep the nose slightly angled out from the rail.

**Step 6:** Grind the length of the rail.

**Step 7:** Use your fingers to twist the nose further over and hit the tail with your rear finger to pop it into the air.

**Step 8:** Land your board with both fingers in the start position.

## *Hang Ten*

Named for a popular surfing move, this usually requires hanging your toes over the edge of the board, but in this variation, you simulate hanging toes.

**Step 1:** Start by putting your index and middle fingers on the board in the classic start position.

**Step 2:** Roll toward a rail.

**Step 3:** Hit the tail of the fingerboard with your rear finger to pop the board up in the air.

**Step 4:** Use the front finger to level out the board and hit the rail with both trucks.

**Step 5:** Grind along the rail and move both fingers to the nose, tipping the board forward into a nose grind.

**Step 6:** Jump your fingers back to the regular position.

**Step 7:** Hit the rear finger down on the tail of the board, popping it in the air.

**Step 8:** Level the board with your front finger and land.

## *Frontside Boneless*

You'll use a basic ledge for this trick, nothing big. It's not exactly a full on grind, but does require a minimum grind along the ledge.

**Step 1:** Put your fingers on the board in the start position.

**Step 2:** Roll toward the ledge at medium speed.

**Step 3:** As you hit the ledge, pop the nose with your front finger.

**Step 4:** Push the board to one side with the rear finger, spinning it 180°.

**Step 5:** Roll away from the ledge.

# Grab Tricks

Grab tricks aren't the easiest when you're working with a fingerboard, since you actually have to grab the board with your fingers. It can be tough to get the hang of, but if you practice, you'll get it.

In most cases, you'll need to pinch two fingers together to hold the board. Which fingers you use will depend on the trick and your own preference. You can even come up with new ways to grab the board.

The other ways you can "grab" a board is by pressing the board flat between your fingers, or grabbing the board lengthwise between two fingers. Pinching with your thumb and index finger can also give you the grip you need to hold onto the board for a minute.

Once you've completed the grab, you'll need to get your fingers back on the deck and land, usually in the same position you started in.

## *Finger Stomp*

Normally, this is referred to as a foot stomp, but since you're using your fingers, we'll call it what it is. This is a quick and easy trick that shows off your grab skills.

**Step 1:** Put your index finger under the board, with your middle finger above, right over the index finger.

**Step 2:** Hold the board between your fingers and lift it.

**Step 3:** Hit the deck with your pinky finger.

**Step 4:** Land the fingerboard and jump your fingers into the starting position.

## *Hand Plant*

This trick is based off of a real size hand plant, but of course, it only uses your thumb. This is usually done on a ramp.

**Step 1:** Put your fingers in the starting position on the board's surface.

**Step 2:** Move quickly toward the ramp.

**Step 3:** Go off the top of the ramp and position your index finger below the board, with your middle finger above it.

**Step 4:** Put your thumb on the ramp, swinging the board up into the air.

**Step 5:** Rotate the board and bring it back to the ramp.

**Step 6:** Land your fingers in the starting position again.

**Step 7:** Roll down the ramp.

## *Christ Air*

If you've played Tony Hawk's Pro Skater, you've probably seen this fun trick being done by Rune Glifberg. Now you can replicate it with your fingerboard, quite easily.

**Step 1:** Put your fingers on the board in the start position.

**Step 2:** Hit the tail of the board with your rear finger to pop it into the air.

**Step 3:** Once in the air, hit the nose of the board with your front finger to push it down fast.

**Step 4:** Use your ring and middle fingers to grab the back of the board and hold it for a second.

**Step 5:** Replace your front finger on the board.

**Step 6:** Use your rear finger to level the board out.

**Step 7:** Land with both fingers in the usual start position.

## *Sacktap*

For this trick, you'll need to start out with an ollie and then do a quick grab. It's actually a pretty simple trick, though it can be tough to actually land with the odd finger positioning.

**Step 1:** Start with your fingers on the board in the start position.

**Step 2:** Hit the tail of the board with your rear finger. You may be rolling or at a standstill, depending on your own preference. The board should pop into the air.

**Step 3:** With the board in the air, use your index and ring finger to squeeze the sides of the board.

**Step 4:** Jump your fingers back on top of the board to land it.

## *Madonna*

With this trick, you will need to get some air time

**Step 1:** Put your fingers in the starting position on the board.

**Step 2:** Roll rapidly along the ground and hit the tail of the board with your rear finger to send it into the air.

**Step 3:** Grab the board with your thumb below it, ring and middle finger on top and your index finger in the air.

**Step 4:** Jump your fingers back on top of the board in the starting position just before landing the board.

## *Crossbone*

You'll recognize this trick from pro skaters. It's a nice simple grab trick , as long as you get into the air.

**Step 1:** Start with your fingers on the board in the beginning position.

**Step 2:** Hit the tail of the board with your middle or rear finger to send it up in the air, similar to an Ollie.

**Step 3:** Let the board tilt at a 45° without leveling it with your front finger.

**Step 4:** Put your thumb on the nose of the board.

**Step 5:** Lift your thumb and slide your front finger forward to level the board out.

**Step 6:** Land the board with both fingers on top in the starting position.

# Verts and Ramp Tricks

Once you have all the basics down, the fun really starts. Now you can start using half pipes and ramps to really spice up your performances. In real life, you might use a pool, actual pipes or concrete/wooden ramps. You can improvise many of these options with your Tech Deck.

Look for curved surfaces and slanted surfaces in your home to use with your fingerboard. You can make your own easily enough with books leaned against other books, or even children's blocks. Look for the arch blocks and turn them upside down for a half pipe.

Again, you can make your own equipment from plaster or concrete and assorted found items. It's surprisingly simple to create your own skate park on moveable pieces of plywood so you can arrange it any way you like. Now you're ready to start in with the tricks!

## *Rail Walk*

A vert ramp is the best place to do this particular trick, but you could also do it on a regular rail if you wanted to.

**Step 1:** Place your fingers on the deck in the starting position.

**Step 2:** Head up the vert ramp.

**Step 3:** Push the nose down with your front finger to pivot once you hit the top of the ramp.

**Step 4:** Spin the board 180° with your rear finger on the tail.

**Step 5:** Switch your finger positions.

**Step 6:** Pivot the board again and let it roll down the ramp.

## *Gap Jump*

You'll need two ramps or verts that are set apart with a little space between them. This gap is what gives the trick its name and makes it possible to jump across the spaces.

**Step 1:** Place your fingers on the board in the starting position.

**Step 2:** Roll rapidly up the ramp.

**Step 3:** Hit the tail of the board slightly with your rear finger and lift the board into the air, jumping the gap.

**Step 4:** Use your front finger to push the front of the board down.

**Step 5:** Ride the ramp back down.

## *Wall Ride*

This is one of the first tricks most finger boarders learn on the ramps, or any vertical wall. It's a fun way to get used to handling the board on anything other than a flat surface.

**Step 1:** Place your fingers onto the deck in the starting position.

**Step 2:** Move toward the vertical surface at regular speed.

**Step 3:** Use your rear finger to tip the nose up.

**Step 4:** Ride the board in an arc across the wall.

**Step 5:** Hit the tail with your rear finger to pop the nose up.

**Step 6:** Drop the nose with your front finger and land.

## *Superman*

When doing this trick with a fingerboard, you can have a lot of fun! It can be done in a forward direction, as well as off a ramp, but you'll probably find it easier to do it off a ramp, because you get more air.

**Step 1:** Place your fingers in the starting position.

**Step 2:** Roll the board up a ramp and launch off the top.

**Step 3:** Keep your rear finger on the board, moving it to the middle. Stick your pointer and ring fingers out as if you were flying.

**Step 4:** Pop your fingers back into the starting position.

**Step 5:** Hit the ramp again and roll back down.

## *The Walk*

This one is kind of like moonwalking, but off a ramp. It's a fun way to show your ramp skills.

**Step 1:** Start with your fingers on the board in the usual position.

**Step 2:** Roll up the ramp at high speed and launch hard enough to get a lot of air.

**Step 3:** "Walk" your fingers by sliding them back and forth as if you're walking on the board.

**Step 4:** Replace your fingers and hit the ramp again.

**Step 5:** Roll down the ramp and stop.

## *Half Pipe Front Flip*

A half pipe is your best option for this, but you can also use a quarter pipe. Make sure you get plenty of air on this one, since you'll need it!

**Step 1:** Place your fingers in the starting position on your board.

**Step 2:** Tip off the top of the half pipe and ride it up the other side. You may need to do this a couple of times before you pick up enough speed to get plenty of air.

**Step 3:** Pop the board further into the air by hitting the back of the board with your rear finger. Your board should be straight up and down.

**Step 4:** Use your whole hand to flip the board around.

**Step 5:** Catch the board and land your fingers in the start position.

**Step 6:** Tilt the board down with your front finger and hit the half pipe again.

**Step 7:** Roll back down and land.

## *Up the Hill*

You'll need a tiny set of stairs to perform this trick, though it can be improvised on a basic incline ramp. See the section on how to make your own stairs . . . it's surprisingly easy and instantly opens up the possibilities for a lot more tricks.

**Step 1:** Place your fingers on the board in the start position.

**Step 2:** Roll the board toward the stairs at medium speed.

**Step 3:** Tap the tail of the board with your rear finger and pop the board into the air.

**Step 4:** Slide your front finger forward to level out the board.

**Step 5:** Land at the top of the stairs with the board and your fingers in the start position and stop the board.

## *Helicopter*

If you enjoy spinning tricks, you'll love this helicopter trick that is done off a vert. It's relatively simple once you get the hang of it.

**Step 1:** Put your fingers on the board in the start position.

**Step 2:** Roll rapidly up the vert and launch it to get some major air.

**Step 3:** Hit the tail of the board with your rear finger and flip the board over so it is resting on your index and middle finger, with the trucks in the air.

**Step 4:** Spin the board around your middle finger.

**Step 5:** Jump your fingers back on top of the board and level it out.

**Step 6:** Land the board on a flat surface.

## *Pong to Pong Blunt*

For something a little more complicated, try this fun trick! It's a good one to surprise and wow your friends.

**Step 1:** Place your fingers on the deck in the start position.

**Step 2:** Move quickly toward a wall.

**Step 3:** As you reach the wall, hit the tail of the board with your rear finger and ollie up the wall as far as possible.

**Step 4:** Hit the tail of the board again with your rear finger and flip the board.

**Step 5:** Land your fingers on the board and guide it to the rolling surface, letting it roll away in fakie position.

## *No Hands Vert*

Ever wanted to fly without using your hands? This trick lets you show off with a "no hands" version of a grab.

**Step 1:** Put your fingers in the start position on the deck of your board.

**Step 2:** Roll rapidly toward your vert and get as much air as possible.

**Step 3:** As soon as you get high enough, put both hands behind your back, leaving the board to fly.

**Step 4:** Wait as long as possible, then land your fingers back on the board in the start position.

**Step 5:** Land the board on the rolling surface if you can.

## *Plaster Flip*

Here's a good, easy trick to learn that requires a vert or similar. You'll need to practice a bit to get it flowing nicely, but it's a good flip.

**Step 1:** Start with your index and middle fingers on the board in the starting position.

**Step 2:** Roll rapidly up the vert.

**Step 3:** When you reach the lip of the vert, hit the tail of the board and move your hand to a 90° angle.

**Step 4:** Pull your fingers back down. The board should flip down.

**Step 5:** Land your fingers in the starting position on the board and guide it back down the vert.

## *Back Stab*

Try this trick as you come off a ramp or vert. It works well in any jump, as well and is unique to fingerboarding.

**Step 1:** Put your fingers on the deck in the start position.

**Step 2:** Roll rapidly toward your vert and go up it, coming off the top at a decent speed.

**Step 3:** Grab the board with the deck in the palm of your hand.

**Step 4:** Form a fist around the board for a moment.

**Step 5:** Let go of the board and land your fingers back on top of it, guiding it down the ramp again.

## *Nose Stall*

Combine this basic trick with any of the others found in this section to create your own sequence of moves that will impress and wow your friends.

**Step 1:** Begin with your fingers in the starting position.

**Step 2:** Head up a vert with some decent speed.

**Step 3:** When you reach the lip, use your front finger to stomp on the board's nose and pop the back up. You'll "stall" the board on the lip of the vert.

**Step 4:** Use your rear finger to press down and drop the board back down again.

**Step 5:** Land the board with both fingers in the required positions.

# Conclusion

Now that you've learned the basics and then some about using finger boards, you can start showing off your amazing new skills. Remember, practice makes perfect. You'll have much better success if you repeat each trick slowly a few times and to make sure that your form is perfect. Then, you can start to speed things up until you have a good flowing motion.

Don't discard this hobby as something to do just when you're bored. There are actual competitions and championships specifically designed for these tiny boards and you could be a part of the next one. With enough practice, anything is possible.

It's also fun to combine the tricks that you've learned here. There's no shortage of combinations you could use to create your very own tricks with your tech deck. Look at what type of trick would logically follow each one in your routine. For example, after an Ollie, a backflip might be a good option, or if you do a nose stall on a vert, you might roll right into a kick flip. The possibilities are endless.

Enjoy your newfound skills!

Made in the USA
Monee, IL
30 October 2020